Making Sense

of Maths

wed
t can
on or by
ry,
ev 7 8QE
1

Picturing data

Paul Dickinson
Stella Dudzic
Frank Eade
Steve Gough
Sue Hough

HODDER
EDUCATION
AN HACHETTE UK COMPANY

The publishers would like to thank the following for permission to reproduce copyright material:

Photo credits: page 5 © Simu Mircea – Fotolia.com; page 6 *t, l* © AFP / Getty Images; page 6 *t, r* © Popperfoto / Getty Images; page 6 *c, l* © Imagestate Media (John Foxx); page 6 *c, r* © Getty Images; page 6 *b, l* © Imagestate Media (John Foxx); page 6 *b, r* © Imagestate Media (John Foxx); page 9 © Imagestate Media (John Foxx); page 18 © Sue Hough; page 27 *all photos* © Sue Hough; page 28 © AFP / Getty Images; page 29 © Sue Hough; page 31 © Martha Mendenhall; page 32 *t* © Imagestate Media (John Foxx); page 32 *c and b* © Sue Hough; page 37 © Sue Hough; page 40 © Sue Hough; page 41 © Ste – Fotolia.com; page 43 *all photos* © Sue Hough; page 44 © Design Pics Inc. / Alamy; pages 46–51 *all photos* © Sue Hough; page 59 © jeff gynane – Fotolia.com; page 61 © Lisa F. Young – Fotolia.com

t = top, *c* = centre, *b* = bottom, *l* = left, *r* = right

All designated trademarks and brands are protected by their respective trademarks.

Every effort has been made to trace all copyright holders, but if any have been inadvertently overlooked, the Publishers will be pleased to make the necessary arrangements at the first opportunity.

Although every effort has been made to ensure that website addresses are correct at time of going to press, Hodder Education cannot be held responsible for the content of any website mentioned in this book. It is sometimes possible to find a relocated web page by typing in the address of the home page for a website in the URL window of your browser.

Hachette UK's policy is to use papers that are natural, renewable and recyclable products and made from wood grown in sustainable forests. The logging and manufacturing processes are expected to conform to the environmental regulations of the country of origin.

Orders: please contact Bookpoint Ltd, 130 Milton Park, Abingdon, Oxon OX14 4SB. Telephone: (44) 01235 827720. Fax: (44) 01235 400454. Lines are open 9.00–5.00, Monday to Saturday, with a 24-hour message answering service. Visit our website at www.hoddereducation.co.uk

© Paul Dickinson, Stella Dudzic, Frank Eade, Steve Gough, Sue Hough 2012

First published in 2012 by
Hodder Education, a Hachette UK company,
338 Euston Road
London NW1 3BH

Impression number 5 4 3 2 1
Year 2016 2015 2014 2013 2012

Cover photo © Juice Images/Alamy
Illustrations by Integra Software Services Pvt. Ltd.
Typeset in India by Integra Software Services Pvt. Ltd.
Printed in Spain

A catalogue record for this title is available from the British Library

ISBN 978 1444 180794

Contents

Chapter 4: Decisions, decisions

Chapter 5: Data collection

Introduction

These books are intended to help you to make sense of the maths you do in school and the maths you need to use outside school. They have already been tried out in classrooms, and are the result of many comments made by the teachers and the students who have used them. Students told us that after working with these materials they were more able to understand the maths they had done, and teachers found that students also did better in tests and examinations.

Most of the time you will be working 'in context' – in other words, in real-life situations that you will either have been in yourself or can imagine being in. For example, in this book you will be looking at how you spend your day, phone usage, Olympic results and The X–Factor, among many other things.

You will regularly be asked to 'draw something' – drawings and sketches are very important in maths and often help us to solve problems and to see connections between different topics. Pictures and diagrams form a large part of the work on collecting, representing, analysing and interpreting data.

You will also be expected to talk about your maths, explaining your ideas to small groups or to the whole class. We all learn by explaining our own ideas and by listening to and trying out the ideas of others.

Finally, of course, you will be expected to practice solving problems and answering examination questions.

We hope that through working in this way you will come to understand the maths you do, enjoy examination success, and be confident when using your maths outside school.

Going to school

1 Below are two examples of a pictograph (sometimes called a pictogram). They show the journeys to school of a class of Year 11 pupils from two different schools.

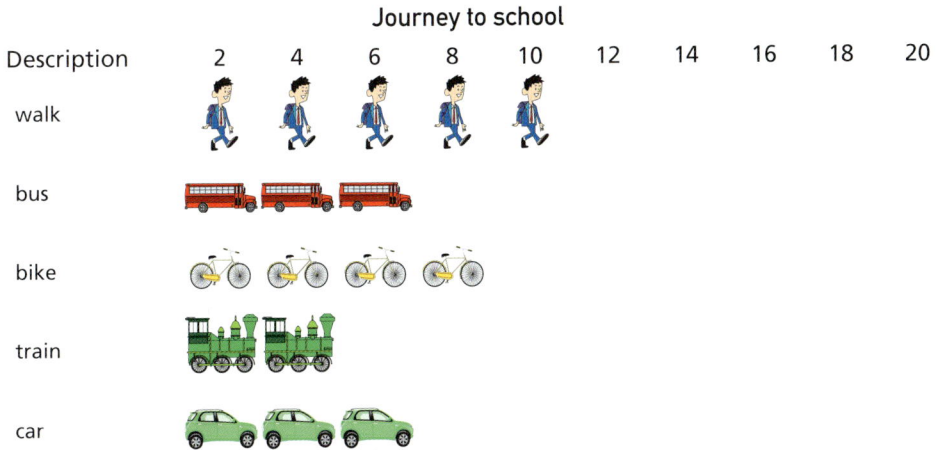

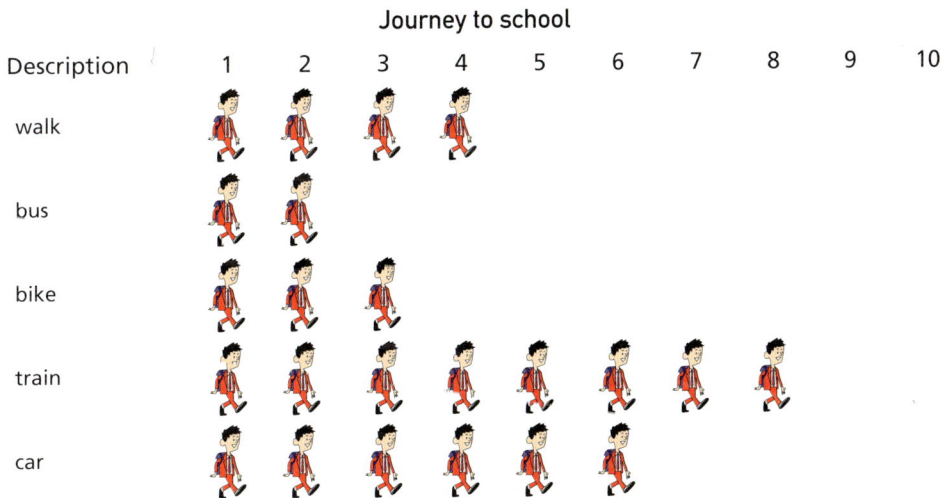

Journey to school

Description	2	4	6	8	10	12	14	16	18	20
walk										
bus										
bike										
train										
car										

Journey to school

Description	1	2	3	4	5	6	7	8	9	10
walk										
bus										
bike										
train										
car										

a) What are the differences in the way the two pictographs have been made?

b) What can you tell about the schools from the two pictographs?

c) Which do you think is the better way of showing this information?

d) How would you improve these pictographs?

e) How many children walked to each school?

2 The pictograph below represents the types of houses that a class of 27 students live in.

Where do you live?

Bungalow	
Caravan	
Detached house	
Flat	
Semi-detached	
Terraced	

Key: Each picture represents the type of home where one person in the class lives

a) How many students live in detached houses?

b) Matthew says that he doesn't think this is a very good way of showing this information. What do you think?

c) Malik suggests that there is an error in the houses pictograph because there are too many houses. Do you think he is correct?

Eat your fruit

3 A group of Year 4 children carried out a survey of their favourite fruits.
Here are two different graphs representing the same information.

Graph 1

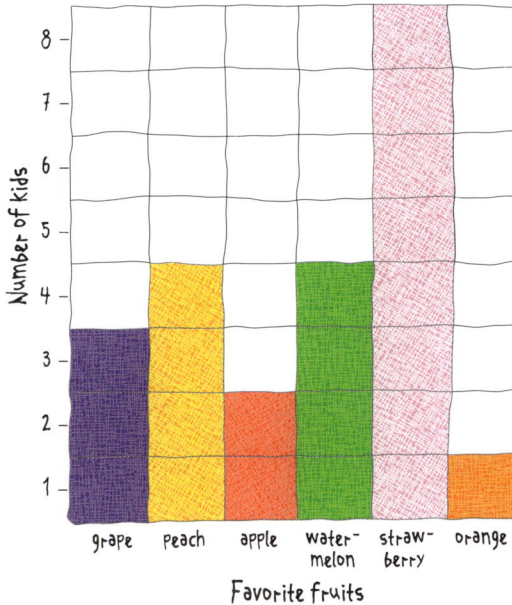

Graph 2

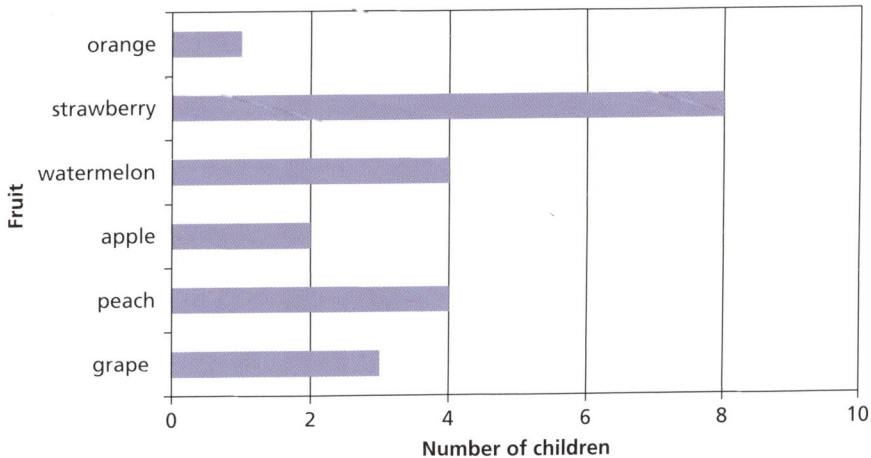

a) Describe some ways in which these graphs are the same and some
ways that they are different.

b) Which do you think is the better graph? Why?

 Turn to page 1 of your workbook and complete Workbook
exercise 1.1.

Mobile phones

4 The data in the table below was collected in 2004 by asking 11 to 16-year-old students to keep a diary of their mobile phone use on a particular day.

Table: Average use of mobile per day by age and gender

Age		11–12		13–14		15–16	
Gender		F	M	F	M	F	M
Average number of calls		2	2	2	1	3	3
Average number of texts		2	10	6	8	13	3

a) What do you think F and M stand for?

b) What does the number 13 tell you?

c) Look at the column 'Age 13–14'. Explain what the 8 and the 1 mean.

d) Do you think older students use their mobiles more, according to this data? Explain.

e) Do boys and girls use their mobiles in different ways according to this data?

5 If the survey was conducted today, how do you think the results would change? Ask members of your class how many calls and texts they made yesterday.

6 a) The data in the table above was used to draw the bar chart below. Find the figures 10 and 1 in the table. Where are they in the bar chart?

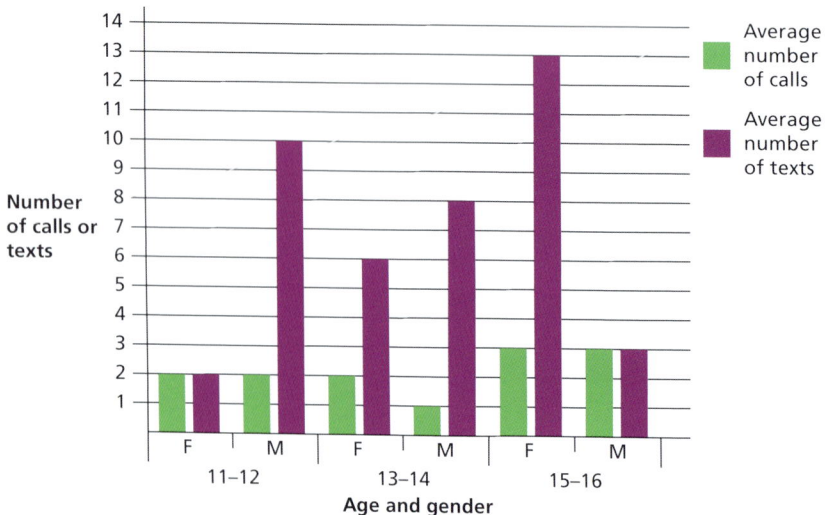

b) Which do you think is easier to understand, the table or the bar chart?

c) What is the advantage of using the table rather than the bar chart?

Turn to page 2 of your workbook and complete Workbook exercise 1.2.

7 The bar chart below shows the most popular applications on mobiles:

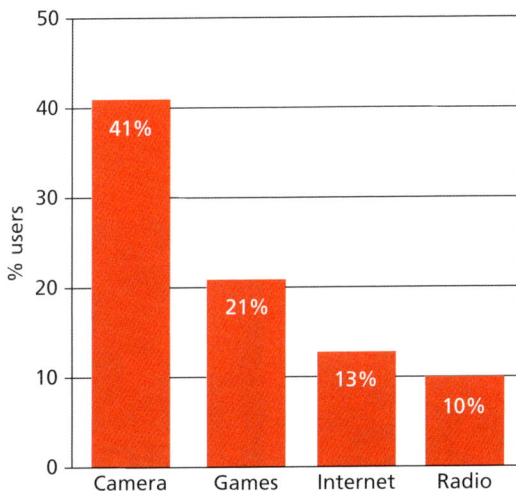

So people use the camera function more than they text.

That's not what it's saying at all!

a) Can you resolve the dispute between these two students?

b) What is your favourite application on your phone?

c) What do you use your phone for most?

d) Why don't the percentages add up to 100%?

How we have changed

8 Michael's granddad was looking at a scrapbook that he had from when he was young.

Here are four famous scenes from it that took place in the last century. Can you identify when these happened?

9 As well as reminiscing about these famous events, Michael's granddad started to think about how tough life was when he was young.

Michael, you don't know how lucky you are! When I was young life was much tougher. Most of our money went on food but you can afford to buy computer games and go to the cinema.

Granddad, it's not as easy as you think. Loads of my income goes on paying the mortgage!

Here is a diagram showing how families spent their income in 1957 and 2006.

Changes in spending in the UK (figures shown as percentages of total household spending)

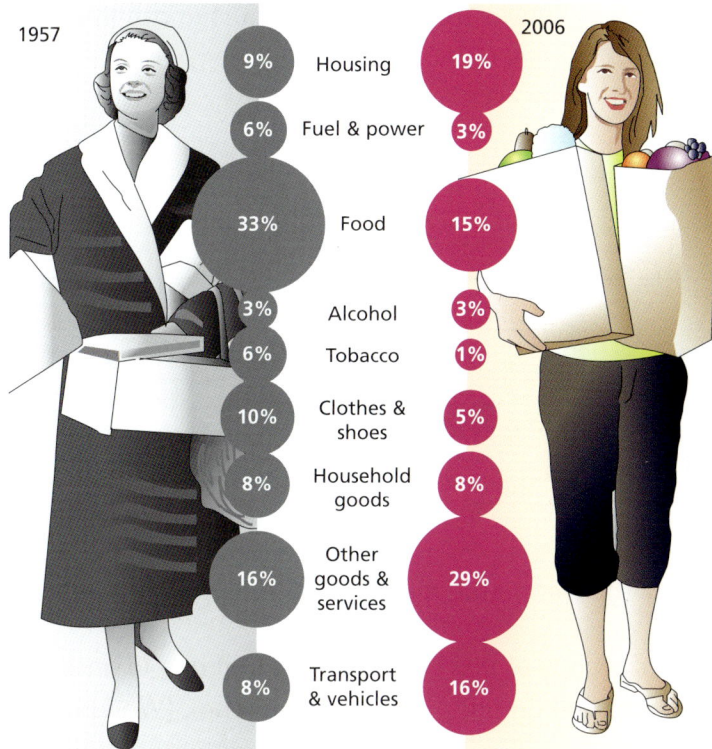

Category	1957	2006
Housing	9%	19%
Fuel & power	6%	3%
Food	33%	15%
Alcohol	3%	3%
Tobacco	6%	1%
Clothes & shoes	10%	5%
Household goods	8%	8%
Other goods & services	16%	29%
Transport & vehicles	8%	16%

a) Was your mother born before or after 1957? How old was your grandmother in 1957?

b) In terms of percentage, what do we spend more on now? Why do you think this is?

c) As a percentage we spend a lot less on food now. Do you think we eat a lot less now than we did in the fifties?

d) As a percentage we also spend a lot less on tobacco. Why do you think this is?

e) Families spend roughly the same percentage of their income on alcohol now as they did in 1957. Do you think this means they drink the same amount now?

f) What do you think 'other goods and services' would include now and in 1957?

g) What do you think fuel and power includes? Why do you think we now spend proportionally less on fuel and power than in 1957?

h) Which of the categories would you describe as 'essentials'? Which would you describe as 'luxuries'?

i) Look back at the photos of Michael and his granddad on page 6. Who do you think was right?

Household spending

10 Michael started to draw a compound bar chart to convince his granddad that things are just as tough now.

How our spending has changed

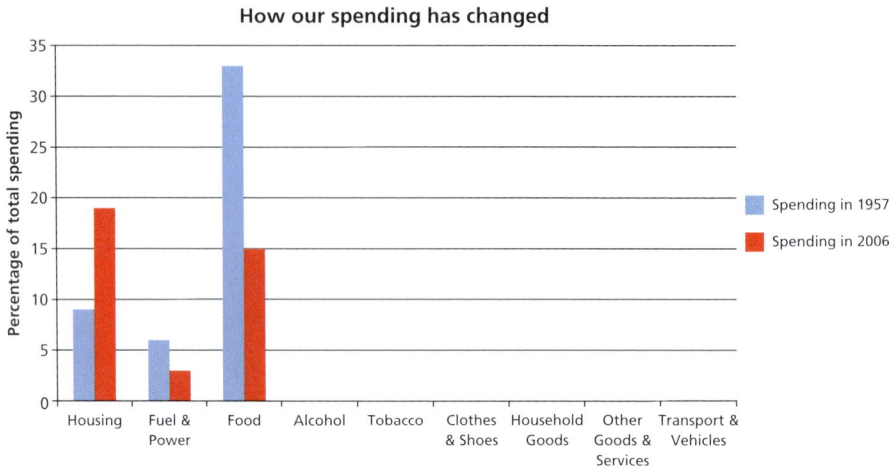

Legend: Spending in 1957 (blue), Spending in 2006 (red)

Categories: Housing, Fuel & Power, Food, Alcohol, Tobacco, Clothes & Shoes, Household Goods, Other Goods & Services, Transport & Vehicles

a) Complete the compound bar chart.

There is a copy of this bar chart you can use to answer **question 10 a)** on page 3 of your workbook (Workbook exercise 1.3)

b) Which do you think is easier to understand, the bar chart or the chart on the previous page?

c) Which one is easier to draw?

d) Which categories show the least change and which show the most?

e) Look at the two graphs below. What do you think they tell us about how much oil and fat we eat (stacked bar chart) and about our fruit consumption (compound bar chart)?

Cooking fats and oils consumption 1950–2000 (grams per person per week)

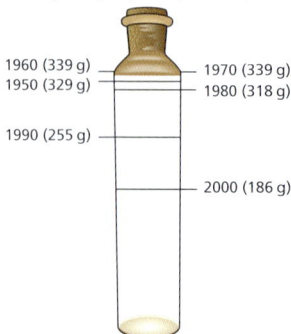

1960 (339 g)
1950 (329 g)
1970 (339 g)
1980 (318 g)
1990 (255 g)
2000 (186 g)

Fruit consumption 1950–2000 (grams per person per week)

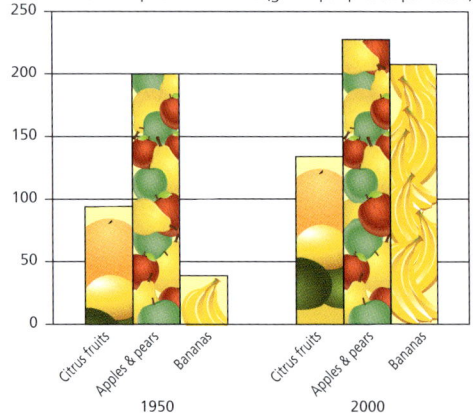

Categories: Citrus fruits, Apples & pears, Bananas (1950 and 2000)

11 Michael's granddad decided to draw a **stacked bar chart** to show the information from page 7. This is shown below.

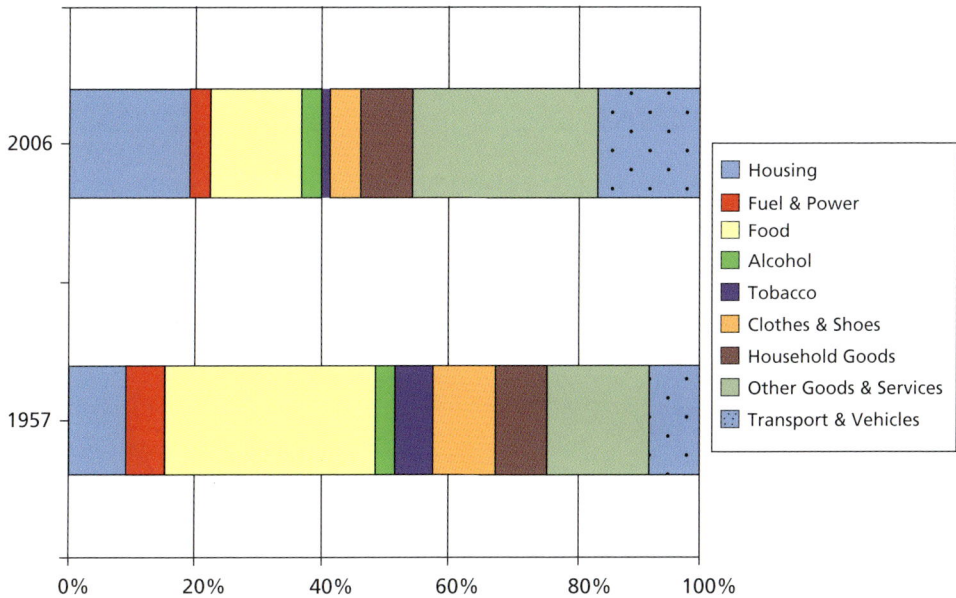

a) Can you see how this was done?

b) Why do you think he made the transport and vehicles part dotted?

c) He said:

> You can see straight away that we spent loads on food and you spent hardly anything.

Do you think this is a better way to show this information than the ways we have seen already?

d) Can you think of any reason why we would draw such a chart?

Turn to pages 4–5 of your workbook and complete Workbook exercise 1.4.

Just a minute

12 A class of 25 students was asked to estimate how long a minute was. Each person was given a stopwatch and asked to close their eyes, start the stopwatch and then stop it when they thought a minute had passed.

Here are the results for the class (recorded to the nearest second):

58, 51, 64, 61, 69, 45, 38, 55, 73, 49, 57, 60, 61, 53, 68, 75, 38, 63, 59, 70, 53, 60, 55, 52, 47

The teacher drew the following diagram on the board:

Stem and leaf diagram showing our class estimates of a minute in seconds

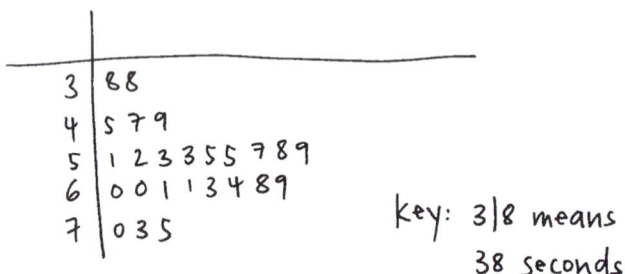

```
3 | 8 8
4 | 5 7 9
5 | 1 2 3 3 5 5 7 8 9
6 | 0 0 1 1 3 4 8 9
7 | 0 3 5
```

key: 3|8 means 38 seconds

a) Describe step by step how you think the teacher drew this diagram.

b) Can you see any advantages of using this stem and leaf diagram rather than just looking at the numbers in a list?

c) Can you see any disadvantages?

13 The group were then told a trick way of counting seconds by saying: 'One elephant, two elephant, three elephant...' and so on. Here are the results for the second test:

57, 52, 64, 59, 67, 54, 60, 56, 49, 64, 65, 60, 56, 62, 54, 70, 66, 53, 49, 66, 58, 60, 62, 52, 55

a) Draw the stem and leaf diagram for these results (note that it helps to put the numbers in order first).

b) How have the results changed?

c) Do you think the class has improved? Explain.

d)

I think the second lot of scores are better because they are not as spread out as the first.

I don't agree because the middle of each of the scores is roughly in the same place.

Who do you think is correct?

e) Find the middle score (median) for both sets of times.

14 The same class of 25 students then had a go at doing a standing long jump. This involved standing with their feet together, jumping forwards as far as possible and measuring the distance in centimetres to their nearest landing point.

Here are their results showing the distance jumped in cm:

90, 132, 86, 105, 72, 112, 99, 101, 146, 135, 122, 68, 107, 115, 88, 131, 140, 95, 108, 113, 126, 94, 105, 118, 140

a) Draw a stem and leaf diagram for these results.

b) Do you think your class would be better or worse at a standing long jump?

c) Collect standing long jump results for your class.

d) Draw a stem and leaf diagram for your class. Then write down three statements comparing your own class with the class above.

Improving learning

15 Teachers often use tests to find out what students have learned. Some teachers test the students before teaching and then again immediately afterwards.

a) Do you think this is a good way of testing how effective the teaching is?

b) Sometimes teachers use the same test before and after. Do you think this is a good idea? Explain your answer.

c) Some people think that this is not a good way to test understanding and memory, because you soon forget what you have learned in lessons. They argue that we should leave a few weeks before testing again. What do you think?

16 Here is an example of a real Year 7 class's results.

Before a class of 26 students were taught reflection in a mirror line, they were tested to find out how much they already knew about the topic. They were then tested again about 6 weeks after teaching using the same test. Here are the results:

Result before teaching:

83, 34, 28, 17, 14, 14, 17, 7, 76, 28, 31, 69, 34, 31, 7, 45, 55, 28, 48, 41, 14, 28

Result after teaching:

97, 38, 69, 31, 31, 48, 31, 34, 79, 34, 59, 100, 55, 66, 24, 76, 79, 45, 79, 62, 52, 41

a) Can you explain why there are not 26 results for each test?

b) Draw a stem and leaf diagram for each of the two tests and decide if the students have improved.

17 Another group of Year 7 students were taught using a teaching approach that focuses on parts that students really struggle with. For example, many students find the question below very hard.

Try this question and compare your answer to those of other students in your class.

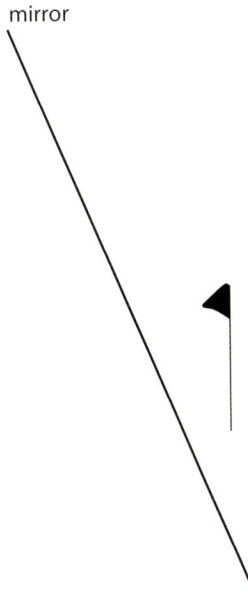

mirror

Where is the image of the flag in the mirror line?

18 Here are the results for the Year 7 class that was taught using the focused teaching approach:

Result before teaching:

88, 62, 46, 4, 31, 23, 31, 50, 27, 77, 35, 46, 81, 27, 65, 35, 88, 62, 65, 38, 50, 50, 35

Result after teaching:

92, 85, 92, 73, 81, 85, 77, 96, 81, 92, 69, 81, 92, 77, 85, 38, 96, 69, 88, 88, 81, 88, 73

Do you think the approach to teaching in **question 16** or the approach in **question 17** is better? Be prepared to give good reasons for your judgement.

Turn to page 6 of your workbook and complete Workbook exercise 1.5.

19 Here is a slightly different bar chart to the one drawn in **Workbook exercise 1.5**. Can you see what is different about it?

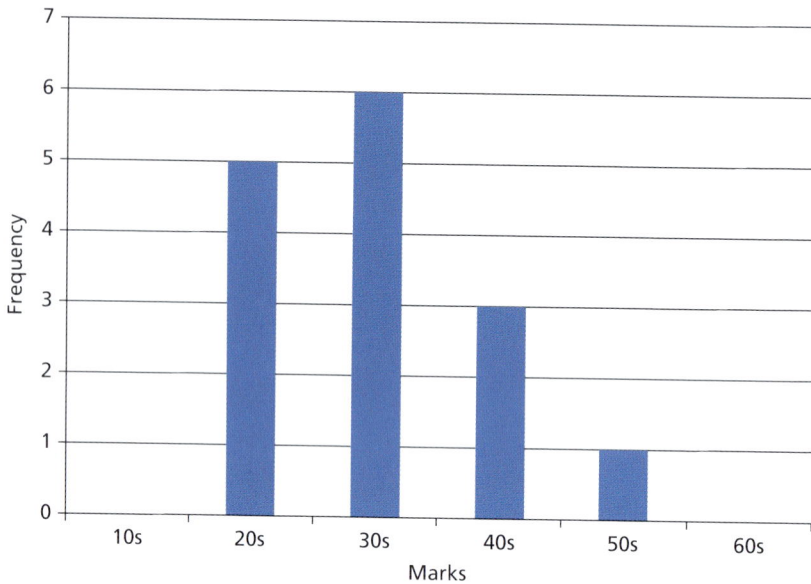

20 If you join the tops of the bars, including the zeros on either side of the bars, then you get what is called a **frequency polygon**.

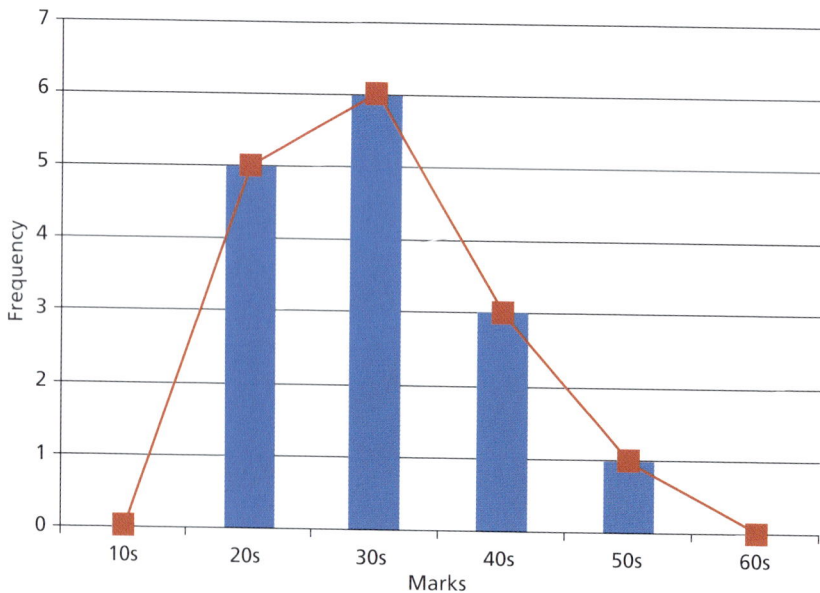

Here is the same frequency polygon with the bar chart removed. Do you think the frequency polygon is a better representation than the bar chart?

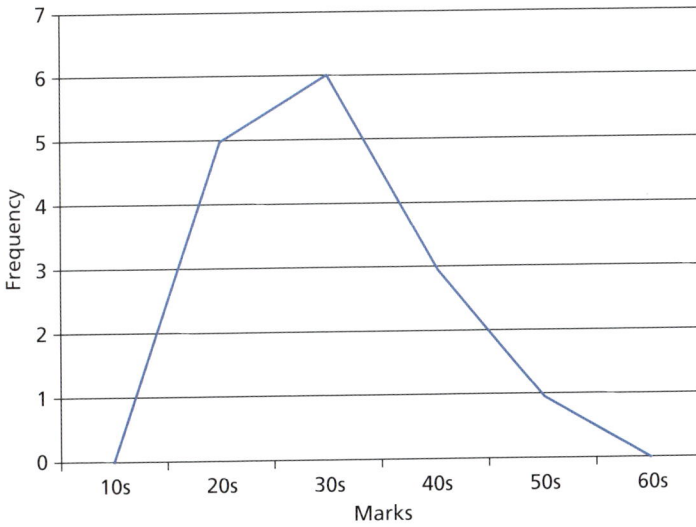

21 Frequency polygons are useful to show visually how things have changed when you try something new, or if you are looking to see if there is a difference between, say, two groups.

Here are the exam marks for two classes. Look at the table of results and the frequency polygon and decide which of the following statements you agree with.

Statement 1: 'The two classes are about the same because most students get between 20 and 50.'

Statement 2: 'Class B is slightly better than A because you can see their marks are just slightly higher.'

Range of marks	Class A	Class B
0–9	0	0
10–19	3	2
20–29	5	5
30–39	8	6
40–49	7	9
50–59	3	4
60–69	2	2
70–79	0	1
80–89	0	0

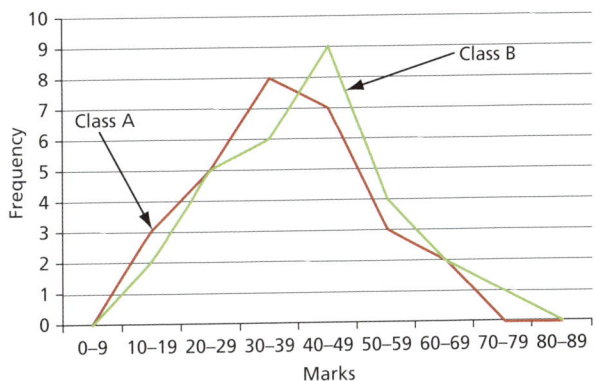

Summary

Below are examples of the different types of charts we have introduced in this chapter.

Favourite pizza toppings	
cheese	🍕 🍕 🍕 🍕 🍕
mushroom	🍕 🍕 🍕 🍕
sausage	🍕 🍕 🍕 🍕 🍕
pepperoni	🍕 🍕 🍕 🍕 🍕 🍕
Key 🍕 = 5 pizzas	

Test scores

9	0 4
8	4 7 9 5 3
7	9 2 0 2
6	8 9 5
5	3 Key: 9|0 means 90

Bar graph 1

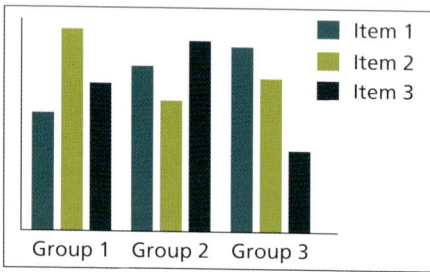

Bar graph 2

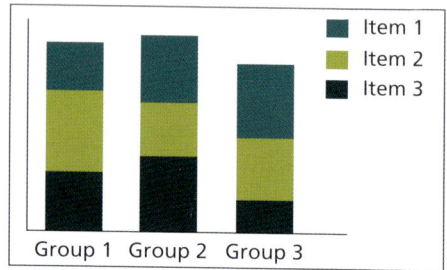

Favourite TV programme

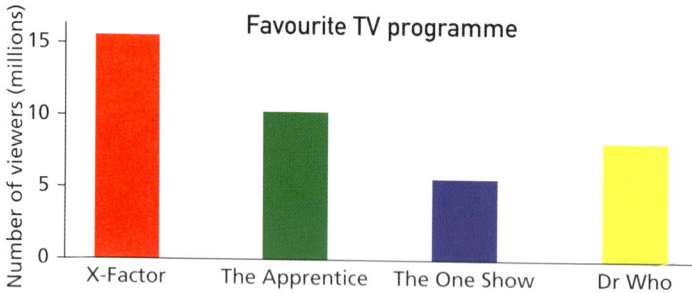

Test scores for geography (out of 200)

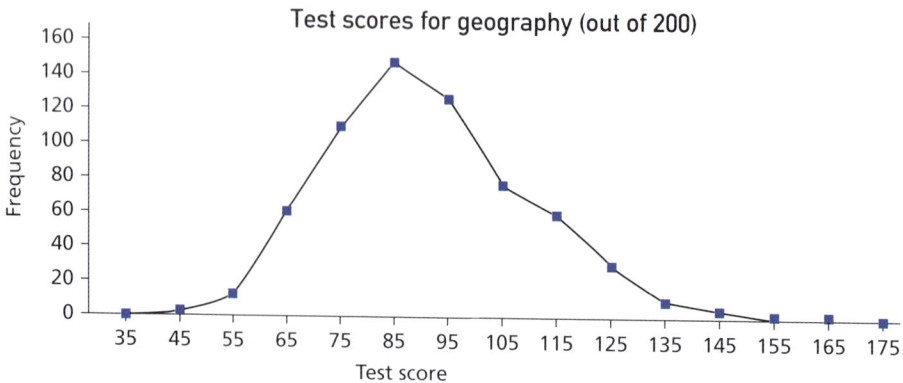

Tables, charts, graphs and diagrams are useful ways of summarising data. You need to make sure that you label the axes, include a proper title and provide a key when necessary.

Games consoles

1 By the beginning of 2010, 18 000 000 games consoles had been sold in the USA. The pie chart shows how many of each type had been sold.

Games consoles sold

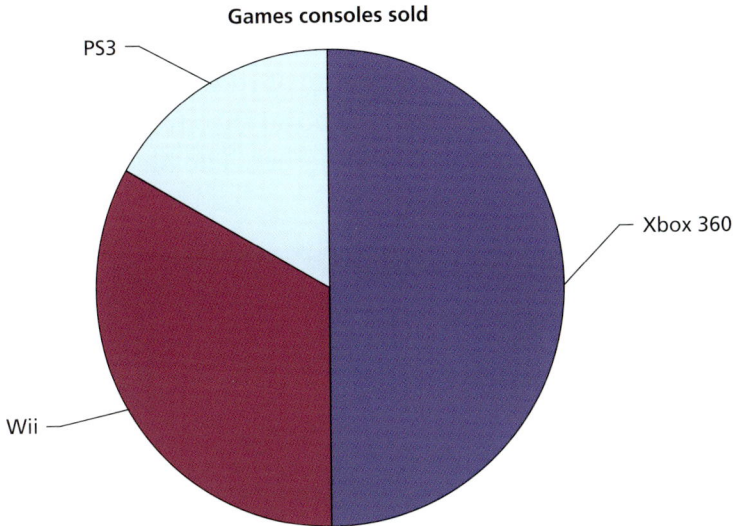

a) Write down three statements about this pie chart.

b) What fraction of sales were of Xbox 360 consoles?

c) How many Xbox 360 consoles was this?

d) About what fraction of sales were of PS3 consoles?

e) How many PS3 consoles was this?

A colourful circle

- You will need 12 multilink cubes: 6 red, 3 black, 2 green and 1 yellow.
- Draw a stacked bar chart showing how many of each colour of multilink cubes you have.
- Now, on plain A4 paper, draw a circle of radius 8 cm.
- Arrange your 12 multilink cubes around the circumference of the circle. The same colours must be together. The pieces of multilink must be equal distances apart.

- Mark points on the circumference halfway between each pair of multilink cubes.
- Join these points to the centre of the circle with a straight line.
- Colour in the segments to match the colour of the multilink cubes.
- How much of the circle is:
  a) red   b) black
  c) green   d) yellow?
- What is the angle at the centre of the circle for the:
  e) red segment   f) black segment
  g) green segment   h) yellow segment?
- If you doubled the number of each colour of multilink cubes, what would happen to the pie chart? Why?
- Check to see if you are correct.

How do you spend your day?

2 **a)** Think about a normal school day. Roughly estimate how many hours a day you spend:

   i) sleeping

   ii) eating

   iii) watching TV

   iv) at school

   v) going out

   vi) other

> There is a blank circle on page 7 of your workbook (Workbook exercise 2.1) which you can use to answer **question 2b)**.

b) Divide up the circle in **Workbook exercise 2.1** to show how you spend your day.

c) The horizontal line on page 9 of your workbook (**Workbook exercise 2.2**) is marked up in hours of the day from midnight to midnight.

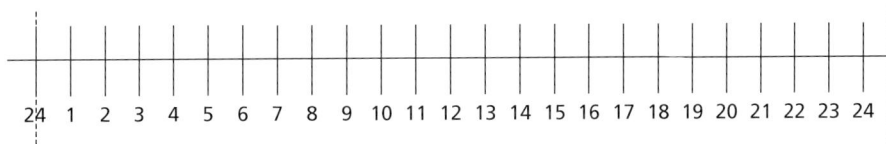

> In your workbook, shade above the line in Workbook exercise 2.2 using different colours to show when you are asleep, eating meals, at school, watching TV, going out, and doing other activities.

   i) Cut out your shaded line by cutting along the dashed lines as shown in **Workbook exercise 2.2**.

   ii) Bend the line into a circle shape, sticking together midnight to midnight.

   iii) Place this ring on a sheet of paper and draw a circle around the ring's outside edge. Mark on the inside of the circle where the different shaded sections begin and end.

   iv) Use these marks to divide up the circle and label the sections.

d) Make three statements comparing this circle diagram with the one you drew in **part b)**.

3 How do you normally spend your time on a Saturday or a Sunday?

> There is a blank circle on page 11 of your workbook (Workbook exercise 2.3) and a line on page 13 of your workbook (Workbook exercise 2.4) which you can use to answer the following questions.

a) Divide up the circle in **Workbook exercise 2.3** to show how you spend one of these days.

b) Shade a timeline in **Workbook exercise 2.4** for the day you selected in the same way as you did in **question 2**.

c) Use your timeline to make a new circle diagram, just as you did in **question 2**.

d) Make three statements comparing the two circle diagrams you have made in **question 3**.

> Turn to page 15 of your workbook and answer the following questions using the circles provided in Workbook exercise 2.5.

4 a) Circle A represents an apple pie. Show how to cut it up to share it equally between six people.

b) A group of ten schoolchildren were asked what their favourite snack was. Four children said chocolate, three said crisps, two said fruit and one said cheese straws. Show how to represent this information in circle B.

c) A group of 16 schoolchildren were asked what their favourite lesson was. Seven children said PE, four said Art, three said Design, one said Maths and one said History.

Show how to represent this information in circle C.

d) A group of 13 teenagers were asked what their favourite hobby was. Four of the group said shopping, three said playing computer games, six said internet use and one said going out. Show how to represent this information on circle D.

e) Conduct some mini surveys of your class and use the remaining circles to display your results.

Surveys

A survey is a way of collecting information. In a survey a lot of people are asked what they think about an issue. A pie chart may be used to present the results of the survey.

5 Students at Kingswood High School were surveyed using the following two questions. 60 students were asked...

Question 1: What make of mobile phone do you have?

Make	Number of students
Nokia	30
Apple	18
Sony Ericsson	6
Samsung	6

Question 2: Which type of charity should the school donate to?

Charity	Fraction of students
Children's	1/3
Cancer	1/6
Animal welfare	1/4
Aids	1/12
The elderly	1/6

 Turn to Workbook exercise 2.6 on page 16 of your workbook. Choose from the four circles provided to answer **questions 5a)** and **b)**.

a) Use one of the circles to draw a pie chart to show which makes of mobile phones students owned.

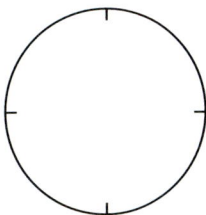
4

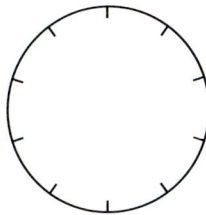
10

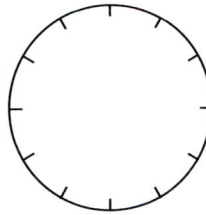
12

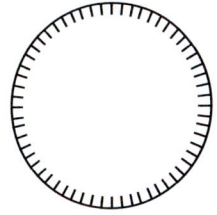
60

b) Use one of the circles to draw a pie chart to show which charities students wanted the school to support.

Money to spend

6 At Kingswood High School the school council had £1000 to spend on improving the school environment. Grace, Harry and Sally decided to conduct a survey to find out what the pupils wanted to do with it. They asked 15 boys and 15 girls from each of the five years in the school.

   a) How many pupils did they ask in total?

   b) Do you think this was a fair way to decide how to spend the money?

7 After carrying out the survey they decided to display the results in charts. They drew three charts and tried to decide which was the best way to show the results. Here are the three charts.

Improving the school - Pie Chart

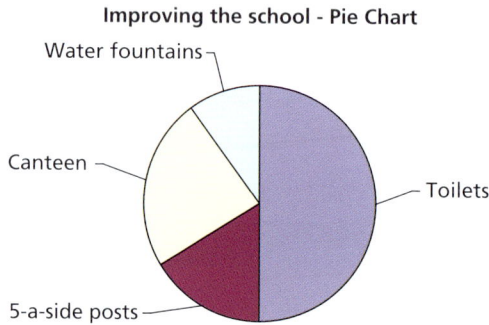

Improving the school - Stacked Bar Chart

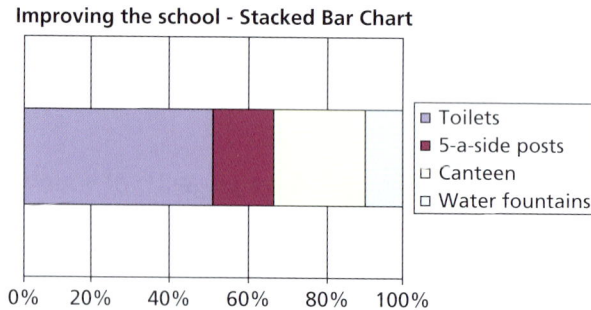

Improving the school - Bar Chart

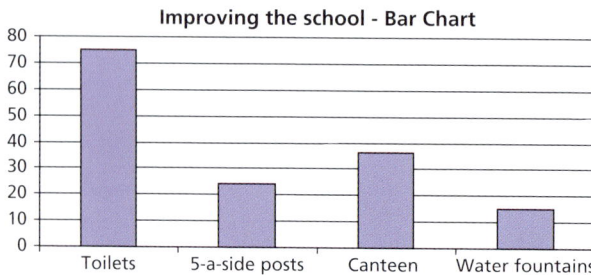

a) Grace thinks the pie chart is best. Give one advantage of displaying the data as a pie chart.

b) Harry thinks the stacked bar chart is best. Give one advantage of displaying the data as a stacked bar chart.

c) Sally thinks the bar chart is best. Give one advantage of displaying the data as a bar chart.

d) In which chart is it easiest to see that half the students want the money spent on the toilets?

e) In which chart is it easiest to see how many students voted for each option?

8 The teachers at the school also had money to spend on their staffroom. The pie chart shows what the 50 teachers wanted to spend the money on.

Pie Chart For Staffroom Spending

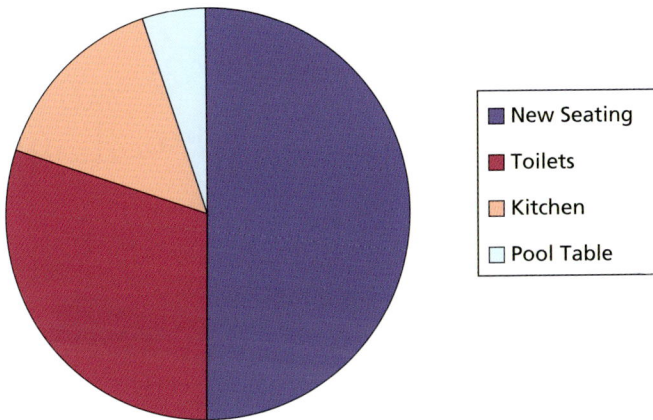

- ■ New Seating
- ■ Toilets
- □ Kitchen
- □ Pool Table

a) Estimate the fraction of teachers who would like the money to be spent on the kitchen.

b) How many teachers is this?

c) Copy and complete the following table to show what the teachers want their money to be spent on.

	Estimated fraction	Number of teachers
New seating		
Pool table		
Toilets		
Kitchen		

Turn to page 17 of your workbook and complete Workbook exercise 2.7.

Drawing a pie chart

To draw a pie chart we use either a protractor or a pie chart scale.

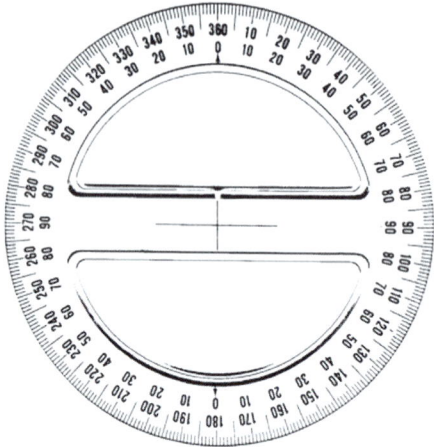

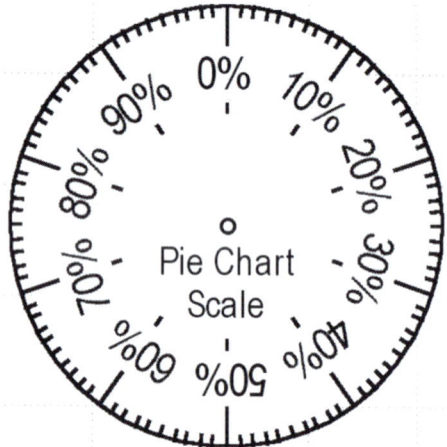

9 Husna wants to draw a pie chart for the following data.

Favourite car	Number of people
Sports car	21
4x4	13
People carrier	12
Limo	4
TOTAL	50

Husna decides she will use a pie chart scale because there are 50 people in her survey. She uses a ratio table to work out what percentage is needed for each car. Here is the start of her ratio table:

Number of People	50	5	1
Percentage of the pie	100%	10%	2%

a) Explain what Husna has done so far.

b) Use Husna's method to draw a pie chart for people's favourite cars.

10 Husna decides to use a protractor to draw a pie chart for the following data.

Favourite fruit	Number of people
Banana	18
Apple	20
Strawberry	20
Grape	15
Pineapple	17
TOTAL	90

a) Why do you think she decided to use a protractor rather than a pie chart scale for this question?

b) Husna uses a ratio table again. This is how she starts:

Number of People	90	9
Angle of the pie	360	36

Explain why '90' and '360' are in the first column.

11 a) Complete Husna's table to find all the angles for the different fruits.

b) Draw a pie chart to show people's favourite fruits.

Student's Book exercise 2.1

1 The table shows the medals won by Spain in the 2008 Olympic Games.

Medal	Frequency
Gold	5
Silver	10
Bronze	3
TOTAL	18

Draw an accurate pie chart to show this information.

2 The table shows the medals won by Brazil in the 2008 Olympic Games.

Medal	Frequency
Gold	3
Silver	4
Bronze	8

Draw an accurate pie chart to show this information.

Summary

Pie charts are used to visualise data or information. In this chapter you worked on interpreting and constructing pie charts.

A pie chart can be an excellent way of communicating information about the number of people picking something or liking something. The whole pie (360°) represents all of the data.

For example, after two days of the London 2012 Olympics, the number of gold medals won by competitors from each continent was as follows:

Continent	Number of gold medals
Asia	14
Africa	1
America	5
Australasia	1
Europe	9

This is how Husna displayed this information in a pie chart:

Total number of gold medals = 14 + 1 + 5 + 1 + 9

= 30

⬇

Number of gold medals	30	3	1	2	4	5	9	14
Angle of the pie	360	36	12	24	48	60	108	168

adding

⬇

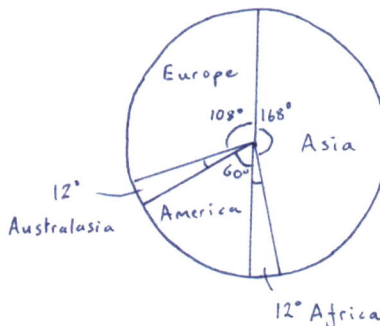

How long is ten seconds?

1 **a)** Work in pairs. Each pair has a stopwatch. Take it in turns to guess how long ten seconds is. One person says 'Go', waits until they think ten seconds have passed, and then says 'Stop'. The other person times this using the stopwatch.

b) Have three goes each at guessing and record all the guesses.

c) In your pair, decide which time you think was the closest and which time you think was the furthest away from ten seconds.

d) Use the first number line in **Workbook exercise 3.1** on page 18 of your workbook and mark on all six guesses.

e) Who was better at guessing? Describe how you can use your number line to help you decide.

2 Adam made four attempts to guess ten seconds. These are the times:

9.43   10.20   9.04   9.88

a) Put these times in order from shortest to longest and describe how you did it. Which is Adam's best guess?

b) Compare your answer to part **a)** with your neighbour's answer.

c) Mark Adam's four guesses on the second number line in **Workbook exercise 3.1** on page 18 of your workbook.

d) Describe where on the number line you can see the closest time and where you can see the time furthest away from ten seconds.

3 Another pair of students had recorded these times as their guesses for ten seconds:

10.23   10.7   10.56   9.75

a) Which is their best guess and which is their worst guess?

b) Mark these four guesses on the third number line in **Workbook exercise 3.1** on page 18 of your workbook.

c) Another student guessed 10.07. Mark this guess on the same number line and decide if it is better or worse than the other four guesses.

4 **a)** How far do you think you could walk in ten seconds?

b) How far do you think you could run in ten seconds?

The closest race

5 **a)** Study the photograph below and write down 3 statements about it.

b) Share your statements with your class.

6 Below are the results of the 2012 Olympics Men's 100 m final:

Men's 100 m Final, Olympic Games 2012

1. Usain BOLT	(JAM)	9.63 sec
2. Yohan BLAKE	(JAM)	9.75 sec
3. Justin GATLIN	(USA)	9.79 sec
4. Tyson GAY	(USA)	9.80 sec
5. Ryan BAILEY	(USA)	9.88 sec
6. Chutandy MARTINA	(FRA)	9.94 sec
7. Richard THOMPSON	(TRI)	9.98 sec
8. Asafa POWELL	(JAM)	11.99 sec

a) Do you think this Olympic final was a close race? Write down a couple of sentences to describe how close you think this race was and justify your comments.

b) Now watch the race in the light of the comments you have just made. The video can be found on YouTube (http://www.youtube.com and search for 2012 Olympics Men's 100 m final).

c) How long does it take you to run 100 m?

7 The first Modern Olympic Games were held in 1896 in Athens, Greece. Below are the results for the men's 100 m in 1896.

Men's 100 m Final, Olympic Games 1896

1. Thomas BURKE	(USA)	12.0 sec
2. Fritz HOFMANN	(GER)	12.2 sec
3. Francis LANE	(USA)	12.6 sec
4. Alajos SZOKOLYI	(HUN)	12.6 sec
5. Alexandros CHALKOKONDILIS	(GRE)	12.6 sec
Thomas CURTIS	(USA)	DNS

Write some comments about this race. Think about how close it was and how it compares with the 2012 race.

8 Isabel is doing a project on the 100 metres. She makes a statement comparing the 1896 race with the 2012 race. Isabel says:

> In 2012 the range of times was 2.36 seconds, whereas in 1896 the range of times was 0.6 seconds. So, I think the 1896 race was quite a lot closer.

a) What do you think about this comment?

b) Describe how you think Isabel worked out her ranges.

9 Isabel uses an app on her phone to make a 'dot plot' of the finishing times for each race.

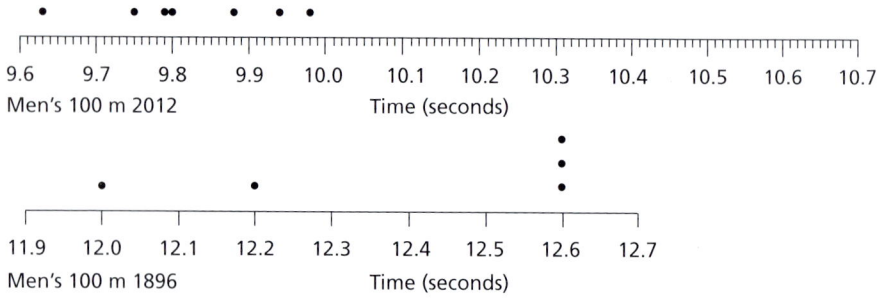

Men's 100 m 2012   Time (seconds)

Men's 100 m 1896   Time (seconds)

a) Do you think she has used the same size of scale to draw each dot plot or not?

b) Why do you think she has marked up one of the scales in hundredths of a second and one of the scales in tenths of a second?

c) How easy is it to compare these races using the dot plots?

d) Make an accurate copy of each dot plot.

e) Show where the winner is on each dot plot.

f) Where can you see the range of times for each race on the dot plots? Mark on each range.

g) Say what the dot plots tell you about how close each race was.

10 a) Go back to the photograph of the 2012 100 metres final and try to match the dots on the dot plot with the lane numbers of the runners.

b) Where can you see the range on the photograph? Is this the same as the range you can see on the dot plot or not?

c) Sketch a finish line and draw stick men to show what you think the end of the race would have looked like in 1896.

Turn to pages 19–23 of your workbook and complete Workbook exercise 3.2.

The longest jump

11 This photograph shows Joy Upshaw-Margerum (USA), who at the age of 46 won the 2007 World Masters Athletics Long Jump Championship with a jump measuring 5.27 metres. Athletes must be 35 or over to enter these championships.

a) What is the furthest you can long jump?

b) What is your school record for the long jump?

c) Mark out these distances, including Joy Upshaw-Margerum's winning distance, in your classroom.

d) Bob Beamon set a world record for long jump of 8.90 m in the 1968 Olympics.
Mark out 8.90 m.

e) At the 2012 London Olympics, UK athlete Greg Rutherford won the long jump by jumping a distance of 8.31 m. Mark out 8.31 m.

f) Bob Beamon's world record stood for 23 years and was finally broken by Mike Powell (USA), who jumped 8.95 m at the 1991 World Championships in Tokyo, Japan. Mark out this distance too.

g) In Chapter 1 you collected your class's results for doing a standing long jump. Mark out some of these distances in your classroom.

Turn to pages 24–27 of your workbook and do Workbook exercise 3.3.

Three exceptional athletes

12 Bob Beamon's (USA) world record for the long jump of 8.90 m stood for 23 years.

Pietro Mennea's (ITA) world record for the 200 metres of 19.72 s stood for 17 years.

Jonathan Edwards' (UK) world record for the triple jump of 18.29 m has yet to be broken, 17 years after it was set in 1995.

These three athletes are exceptional in that not only did they each achieve a world record in their event, but in each case it was several years before their world record was broken. Such exceptional results are sometimes referred to as **outliers**.

Look back at your class results for a standing long jump. Are there any exceptional results which might take a long time to beat?

Turn to pages 28–32 of your workbook and have a go at Workbook exercise 3.4.

13 Isabel is discussing her Olympics project with Charlie. She is trying to decide whether men are improving at long jump or not. Isabel says:

> Nobody at the Olympics has jumped anywhere near Bob Beamon's jump of 8.90 m, so I don't think the men are improving.

Charlie says:

> Bob Beamon's was an exceptional jump that was out of sync with jumps that had gone before. It's misleading to just look at the winner's jumps. I think it would be better to look at the middle person's jump.

Isabel thought it would be a good idea to draw a dot plot for each set of results and put them underneath each other.

Charlie said that would take a long time because there were lots of results. In the end they decided to look at the results every 8 years from 1960 to 2008. This goes from before Bob Beamon's jump up to recent times.

Charlie said he thought that they should just plot the highest, the lowest and the middle result for each year.

This is what Charlie drew for the 1960 results:

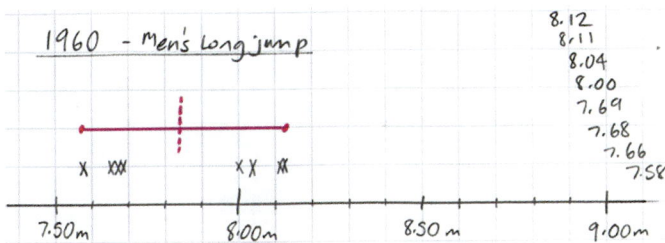

Isabel was confused. She said: 'I can see where to start and finish your line, but how do you know where to put the dotted line?'

Charlie explained: 'What I do is pair off the results starting from the ends. Here I got down to two results in the middle, so I go in the middle of those. This finds me the middle result, which is called the median.'

a) Check how Charlie's method works to find the middle result.

b) What is the median (middle) result for the 1960 long jump?

c) Sometimes athletes test positive for drugs after taking part in a competition. This can lead to them being disqualified and stripped of their medal. If the 1960 winner had been disqualified, what differences would this have made to Charlie's diagram and to the median?

Turn to pages 33–35 of your workbook and complete Workbook exercise 3.5.

Is my teaching getting better?

14 Miss Jones qualified as a dance teacher in 2009 and opened her own dancing school the same year.

To encourage students to join her dancing school, Miss Jones started off by making sure her fees were lower than at other dancing schools in the local area. Now, after four years, Miss Jones wants to increase her fees and update her website. She would like to be able to make a claim about how the results for her classes have improved since she first opened her school. She prints off the marks for her grade 1 ballet classes for the last four years and wonders how to analyse them.

Here are the results:

Year	Marks
2009	78%, 92%, 76%, 90%
2010	84%, 84%, 82%, 78%, 87%
2011	78%, 90%, 90%, 72%, 80%, 85%, 88%, 87%
2012	88%, 82%, 84%, 82%, 82%, 88%, 87%, 81%, 83%, 86%, 86%

The grading system for the IDTA ballet exams is as follows:

Pass 65–74%	Commended 75–79%	Highly commended 80–84%	Honours 85% +

a) At a glance would you say these marks are improving or not?

b) Miss Jones starts by looking at the highest mark for each year and the median mark for each year. Could she make a claim about improvement using either of these results?

c) Suggest some other ways in which Miss Jones could analyse these marks.

d) Choose one of these suggestions and see what conclusions you could make.

When comparing sets of data, it is sometimes helpful to choose one value to represent the whole set of data. In the case of a competition, we are often interested in the winner's result.

Sometimes the winner's result is so far above the rest of the group that it does not really give a true picture of how the whole group performed.

Another result that can be useful to consider is the median (the middle person's value). The **median** can give a fairer picture of how the group as a whole performed, because it ignores any outliers.

The class Olympics

Here are some suggestions for data collection for your class:

- How long can you stand on one leg with your eyes closed?
- How many jumps can you do in a minute?
- How high up a wall can you reach if you jump?
- How many different four-legged animals can you name in 1 minute?
- How far can you throw a netball?
- Estimate the length of a line drawn on the board by your teacher.

For each activity:

1) Split your class into two groups (for example boys v girls) and write down a prediction, with a reason, about which group you think will perform better.
2) Try each activity and collect the results for every student in your class.
3) For each group, use the data collected to draw a dot plot, find the range and find the median.
4) Write a few sentences saying what the dot plot, the range and the median tell you about each group's performance.
5) What does it tell you if one group has a larger range than another group?

Food glorious food

15 It is claimed that crisp consumption in Britain is higher than in any other European country, and that Brits on average eat three packets of crisps a week. Crisp consumption is said to be highest in teenagers than in any other age group.

In order to test these claims, Shez and Helena decided to collect some data from their school. First they asked the people in their class how many packets of crisps they ate in a week. Then they asked their teachers the same question.

They then drew two pictographs to show the results.

Pupil A	🟦🟦🟦🟦🟦
Pupil B	🟦🟦🟦🟦🟦🟦🟦🟦🟦🟦
Pupil C	🟦🟦🟦
Pupil D	🟦🟦🟦🟦🟦🟦
Pupil E	🟦🟦🟦🟦🟦🟦🟦🟦🟦🟦🟦🟦
Pupil F	🟦🟦🟦🟦🟦
Pupil G	🟦🟦🟦🟦🟦🟦
Pupil H	
Pupil I	🟦🟦🟦🟦🟦🟦🟦🟦🟦
Pupil J	🟦
Pupil K	🟦🟦🟦
Pupil L	🟦🟦🟦🟦🟦

Key: 🟦 represents one bag of crisps

Teacher 1	🥔 🥔 🥔 🥔 🥔 🥔 🥔
Teacher 2	🥔 🥔
Teacher 3	🥔 🥔 🥔 🥔 🥔
Teacher 4	
Teacher 5	🥔
Teacher 6	🥔 🥔 🥔 🥔 🥔 🥔 🥔 🥔 🥔 🥔 🥔 🥔 🥔 🥔
Teacher 7	🥔 🥔 🥔 🥔
Teacher 8	🥔 🥔
Teacher 9	
Teacher 10	🥔 🥔 🥔
Teacher 11	🥔 🥔 🥔 🥔
Teacher 12	🥔 🥔 🥔 🥔 🥔 🥔 🥔 🥔
Teacher 13	🥔 🥔 🥔 🥔 🥔
Teacher 14	🥔 🥔 🥔
Teacher 15	🥔 🥔 🥔 🥔 🥔 🥔 🥔 🥔 🥔
Teacher 16	🥔

Key: 🥔 represents one bag of crisps

Shez said: 'I think the teachers are eating more bags on average. One teacher is having as many as two bags a day.'

Helena said: 'I think it's the students who are eating more. Quite a few teachers have three or less bags a week whereas there are hardly any pupils eating such small quantities.'

What do you think? Which group is eating more crisps on average?

16 Helena decided to redraw the graphs in order to see how many packets are eaten on average. She started with the pupils' graph as shown:

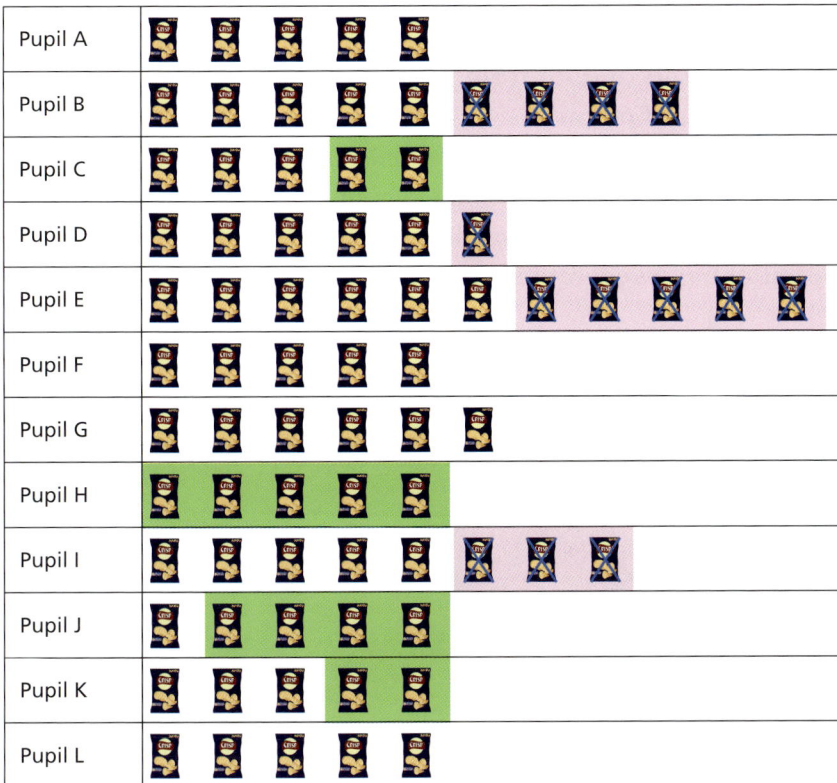

Pupil A											
Pupil B											
Pupil C											
Pupil D											
Pupil E											
Pupil F											
Pupil G											
Pupil H											
Pupil I											
Pupil J											
Pupil K											
Pupil L											

Write a description of what Helena has done.

Turn to page 36 of your workbook and do the same for the teachers' graph in Workbook exercise 3.6.

17 **a)** Helena reckoned that on average the pupils had about five bags of crisps a week and the teachers had about four bags. Describe where you can see these numbers in the redrawn pictographs.

b) Shez worked out the pupil average by counting the total number of bags of crisps (62) and dividing by the number of pupils (12). If you were to bring all the pupils in a room with their crisp packets, describe what 62 ÷ 12 would look like.

c) How does Shez's method for finding the average differ from Helena's method? How is it the same?

d) In this survey both the pupils and the teachers were found to eat more bags of crisps a week than the national average of three bags a week. Suggest some reasons as to why this may be the case.

Class activity 3

Healthy eating?

1 Collect three sets of data from your class:
   a) the number of pieces of fruit eaten per week
   b) the number of portions of vegetables eaten per week
   c) the number of bars of chocolate eaten per week
2 In each case draw a pictograph and use it to find the average amount of fruit/vegetables/chocolate bars eaten per person per week.
3 What does this tell you about the healthy eating habits of your class?

The charity event

18 In order to raise some money for charity, Celia and three of her friends decide to pool any spare money they have in their pockets at afternoon registration. They then redistribute the money equally between them, so that each of their chosen charities receives the same amount each day.

They do this for a whole week.

a) Imagine if you and three of your friends did this today. How much money would each of your charities get?

b) Look at the record Celia has made of the money she and her friends donated.

| Day | Amount donated by each person | | | |
	Celia	Tracy	Sue	Helen
Monday	£1	50p	20p	60p
Tuesday	40p	£4	£2	20p
Wednesday	26p	70p	70p	50p
Thursday	£2.06	20p	12p	42p
Friday	Absent	76p	£1	£1.90

Celia thinks that they should share out the money each day. Tracy thinks it would be better to collect all the money together and share it out at the end of the week. Working in pairs, one person follow Celia's suggestion to share out the money and the other use Tracy's method. See whether this makes a difference to the overall outcome.

c) Which people's charities will benefit from sharing out the donations and which people's charities will lose out?

Finding the mean

19 The mean is a type of average that you are probably familiar with. In this question you will look at two different ways of finding the mean.

Five pupils were asked how many portions of chips they eat in a week.

They replied as follows: 7 5 5 1 0

Method 1 for finding the mean:

$$7 + 5 + 5 + 1 + 0 = 18$$

$$18 \div 5 = 3 \, r \, 3$$

Method 2 for finding the mean:

Pupil 1
Pupil 2
Pupil 3
Pupil 4
Pupil 5

a) Copy the picture for method 2 and show how to balance out the portions of chips.

b) Do the methods give the same answer?

c) Compare the methods. For example, where can you see the total of 18 in the picture? How does 'divided by' compare with what you did with the picture?

d) Make up a story involving portions of chips and pupils to describe what happens in method 1.

e) Make up a story involving portions of chips and pupils to describe what happens in method 2.

20 Vicky comes to college wearing a new pair of leather gloves. Her friends take it in turns to try the gloves on. They soon realise that one size does not fit all. They decide to measure the length of their middle fingers in millimetres.

The results are as follows:

76   82   65   90

Method 1 for finding the mean:

$$76 + 82 + 65 + 90 = 313$$
$$313 \div 4 = 78 \cdot 25$$

Method 2 for finding the mean:

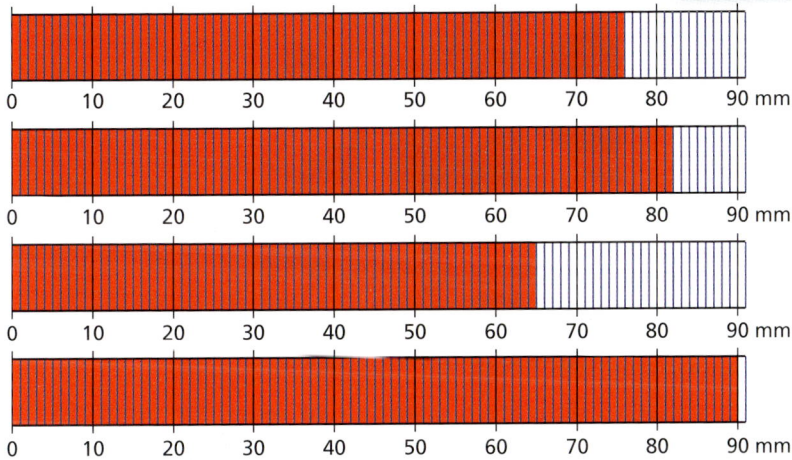

a) Describe how you could use the pictures in method 2 to help you average out the middle finger length.

b) Do the methods give the same answer?

c) Compare the methods. For example, where can you see the total of 313 in the picture? How does 'divided by' compare with what you did with the picture?

d) Make up a story involving fingers and people to explain method 1.

e) Make up a story involving fingers and people to explain method 2.

✏️ Turn to pages 37–43 of your workbook and complete Workbook exercise 3.7.

The typical student

21 **a)** What do you think are the characteristics of a typical Year 10 student from your school?

b) Look around the room and think about the students in your form to help you predict the profile of a typical male and typical female in terms of:

  A) hair colour
  B) favourite colour
  C) number of brothers/sisters
  D) height
  E) Key Stage 3 Maths level

22 Matt and Amy collected data from a sample of Year 10 students in their school. They used this data to draw up a profile for the average Year 10 male and the average Year 10 female in their school.

Use the data they collected (see **Workbook data sheets 3.8** and **3.9** on pages 44 and 45 of your workbook) to make a profile for the average Year 10 male and average Year 10 female in their school.

Which type of average should I use?

23 Look back at the methods you used to make the Year 10 student profiles in **question 22**. For each category, indicate whether you used:

a) the mean

b) the median

c) the mode

d) another method to find the average values

24 **a)** Imagine that you were teaching somebody about the mean, median, mode, average and range. Write down your own explanation of what each word means.

b) Give an example of how to find each of the values listed in **part a)** using data from this chapter. Alternatively you could collect some data of your own to use in your examples.

c) In a class of 22 Year 10 pupils, ten pupils had brown eyes, seven pupils had blue eyes and five pupils had green eyes.

   i) Can you find the modal eye colour for this class? Why or why not?

   ii) Can you find the mean eye colour for this class? Why or why not?

   iii) Can you find the median eye colour for this class? Why or why not?

Summary

In this chapter you have looked at sets of data and considered:
- How spread out the data is
- How to choose a single value to represent a set of data

Looking at the data as a whole

The **dot plot** is a good way of displaying data. The dot plot below shows the finishing times for the Women's 100 m at the London 2012 Olympics:

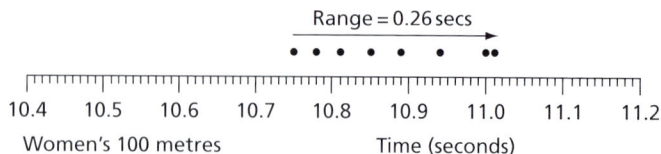

Range = 0.26 secs

10.4   10.5   10.6   10.7   10.8   10.9   11.0   11.1   11.2

Women's 100 metres   Time (seconds)

You can see how spread out or bunched up the data is.

You can see the **range** (the gap between the shortest and longest finishing time). The dot plot helps you put the data in order, which is important if you want to find the **median**.

If you want to compare 2 sets of data (e.g. the women's 100 m with the men's 100 m) then the dot plots can help you see similarities and differences at a glance.

Representing the data with a single value

Sometimes you might want to come up with a value which typically represents a set of data. One way to do this is to find an average value. There are 3 types of average: the **mean**, the **median** and the **mode**.

Here are 5 people who work in an office:

If you were asked to describe a typical person who worked in this office you might say they were brown–haired and brown–eyed. Here you would be looking at the hair colour and eye colour which are most common. The item which occurs the most is called the mode.

The figures below show the number of chocolate bars eaten in a week by people in the office

      0   2   20   4   2

If you wanted to claim that that the people in the office were healthy eaters you might choose to quote the mode or the median number of chocolate bars eaten per week.

You would probably not choose the mean in this case; the mean amount of chocolate bars eaten would seem quite high when you have balanced out the 20 bars eaten by one person between all 5 people.

The mobile phone revolution

1 A search of mobile phone surveys reveals the following:

- Messaging is the fastest growing segment of the mobile communication industry (Nokia 2002).
- Young people are the driving force behind the texting revolution (Reid and Reid 2004).
- 80% of 14–16-year-olds own their own mobiles (NOP 2001).
- One-third of teens in the US text more than 100 times a day (Pew 2010).
- Girls send and receive more than twice as many text messages a day as boys (Pew 2010).
- 64% of parents look at the contents of their teenagers' mobile phones, with 62% of parents having taken away a phone as a form of punishment (Pew 2010).
- People in the UK are now more likely to text than to make a phone call (Ofcom 2012).
- While 58% of people communicated via texts on a daily basis in 2011, only 47% made a daily mobile call (Ofcom 2012).

For each of the statements above, write down:

a) whether or not you think the statement is still true (some are from quite old surveys)

b) how you would go about collecting data to see whether or not the statement is still true.

Are you a texter or a talker?

2 Which, if any, of the statements in **question 1** would help you to answer the question: 'Are people texters or talkers?'

3 Matt and Amy decide to survey their Year 9 form group to find out how much students use their phones for texts and for calls. They hand out copies of the following questionnaire:

Name: _____   Form: _____

Please answer the following questions as accurately as possible:

1) How many phone calls have you made in the last 24 hours (this can include calls you have made on your land line)?

   _____

2) How many text messages have you sent in the last 24 hours?

   _____

Thank you for filling in this survey.

Matt and Amy sit at a computer and collate the results of the survey. Amy reads them out, while Matt records them in the following way:

Year 9 – Number of phone calls made in one day

2,	1,	3,	6,	0,	1,	8,	0,	2,	10,		
0,	0,	1,	0,	9,	2,	1,	1,	1,	3,		
1,	3,	6,	3,	4,	2,	1,	4,	3,	5,	2,	2

Year 9 – Number of text messages sent in one day

0,	0,	8,	5,	0,	45,	0,	0,	1,	0,		
2,	4,	50,	0,	0,	1,	5,	3,	2,	102,		
4,	19,	5,	0,	1,	0,	1,	1,	6,	11,	2,	3

a) Spend a minute studying this data and make a statement based on what you see. Be prepared to justify your statement to your classmates.

The data collected by Matt and Amy is shown in Workbook exercise 4.1 on page 46 of your workbook. Use this to answer part b).

b) Find the total number of calls made and texts sent by the Year 9 class.

c) Describe and demonstrate your methods to your class.

d) Matt decides to use two different methods to help him find the totals. This is what he does to find the total number of messages sent.

Year 9 - Number of text messages sent in one day

$$0, \; 0, \; 8, \; 5, \; 0, \; 45, \; 0, \; 0, \; 1, \; 0,$$
$$2, \; 4, \; 50, \; 0, \; 0, \; 1, \; 5, \; 3, \; 2, \; 102,$$
$$4, \; 19, \; 5, \; 0, \; 1, \; 0, \; 1, \; 1, \; 6, \; 11, \; 2, \; 3$$

$$\overline{6 \;\; 23 \; 63 \;\; 5}_{\;\;98} \;\big|\; \overline{1 \;\; 46 \;\; 6}_{\;\;57} \;\big|\; \overline{4 \;\; 9 \;\; 113}_{\;\;127} \;\; S \;\big|$$

$$260 + 22 = \boxed{282}$$

$$
\begin{aligned}
0 - 10 &= 0 \\
1 - 5 &= 5 \\
2 - 3 &= 6 \\
3 - 2 &= 6 \\
4 - 2 &= 8 \\
5 - 3 &= 15 \\
6 - 1 &= 6 \\
7 \times \;\; &\overline{46}
\end{aligned}
\qquad
\begin{aligned}
8 - 1 &= 8 \\
&\;11 \\
&\;19 \\
&\;45 \\
&\;50 \\
&\;102 \\
&\;\overline{235} \\
&\;\cancel{12}
\end{aligned}
$$

$$46 + 235 = \boxed{281}$$

Write a description of exactly what you think he did for each method.

e) Find the calculation:

$$5 - 3 = 15$$

Where can you see this in his first method?

f) Matt has obviously made a mistake in one of his calculations. Where is this mistake?

4 Use what you have done so far to help you write a statement comparing text use with call use for this Year 9 class.

5 Amy makes the following statement:

On average, teenagers text nearly three times as much as they phone.

Matt thinks this is a rather sweeping statement to make. In what ways would you agree or disagree with Amy's statement?

6 Matt says:

We only asked Year 9 pupils. I think it could be even more. My sister in Year 11 is texting all the time, whereas my brother in Year 7 hardly uses his phone at all. We need to ask a range of ages of teenagers.

The next day they get two Year 11 classes to fill in their questionnaire.

Amy collates the results in the following way:

Number of phone calls made in one day	
Number of calls	Number of students
0	5
1	4
2	3
3	6
4	2
5	3
6	1
7	0
8	1

Number of text messages sent in one day	
Number of texts	Number of students
0	4
6	5
7	1
10	2
12	3
17	1
20	2
23	1
30	2
35	1
51	1
53	1
210	1

Matt looks at these tables.

He says: 'I don't understand what these mean.'

What might the raw data have looked like, as Amy read it off each questionnaire? Make a possible list for both the texting and the phoning.

7 **a)** Make some statistical statements comparing text use with phone use for the Year 11 class. Try to use the words mean, median, mode and range to help you compare the data.

b) Which of the averages (mode, median, mean) do you think best represents the Year 11 data?

> Many people find it hard to imagine what the raw data looked like once it is presented as a table or graph. Sometimes it helps to think about how you would have collected the data originally and then to create a possible list of the original data.

You could now try Workbook exercise 4.2 on page 47 of your workbook.

Good at spelling?

8 Marcus's mum wants to encourage her son to be a good speller. Whilst he is in Year 5, she keeps a record of his spelling test marks on a chart on the kitchen wall. This is what it looks like:

Marks out of 10	0	1	2	3	4	5	6	7	8	9	10
How often					II	III	HHT HHT I	HHT IIII	HHT	HHT II	IIII

a) Describe how you think the data was collected.

b) Write down what you think the raw data could have looked like.

c) Calculate the mean, median, mode and range for the data.

d) If you were Marcus, which average (mean, median or mode) would you use to convince your mum that you were doing well with your spelling?

e) Marcus's friend Adam has a range of 8 for his marks. He says this means that he's doing better than Marcus because he has a higher range. Do you agree with Adam? Explain your answer carefully.

A negative manager?

9 In 2009 and 2010 there was a lot of discussion in the press about the negative style of play adopted by the multi-million pound football team at Manchester City. A keen supporter wants to compare ex-manager Mark Hughes's record with that of the manager who replaced him, Roberto Mancini.

Here are the two tables of data the supporter produced:

Manchester City under Mark Hughes (18/08/09 to 16/12/09)

Number of Goals	Number of Games
0	ΙΙ
1	ΙΙ ΙΙ Ι
2	Ι ΙΙ Ι
3	Ι ΙΙ Ι
4	Ι
5	
6	
7	

Manchester City under Roberto Mancini (19/12/09 to 09/05/10)

Number of Goals	Number of Games
0	ΙΙ ΙΙ ΙΙ
1	ΙΙ Ι Ι
2	ΙΙ Ι Ι
3	ΙΙΙ
4	ΙΙΙ
5	Ι
6	Ι
7	

a) Describe how you think the supporter collected this data.

b) Write down what you think the raw data could have looked like.

c) Use the data to help you decide under which manager City were more negative (scored fewer goals on average). Then write a brief report for a newspaper that discusses your findings.

Now answer the questions in Workbook exercise 4.3 on pages 48–49 of your workbook.

How easy is it to estimate time?

10 Ms Linnecor's and Mr Norton's Year 7 classes challenged each other to find out who was the best at estimating a minute. The bar charts shown below were drawn from the data they collected.

Ms Linnecor's class:

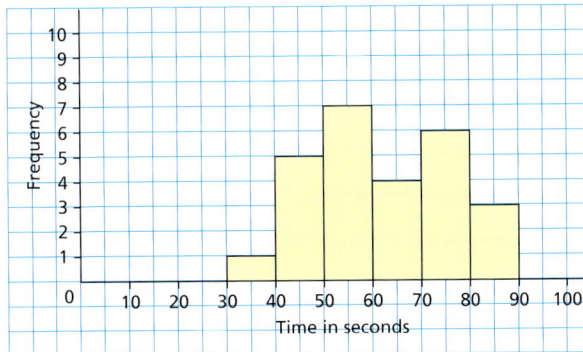

Mr Norton's class:

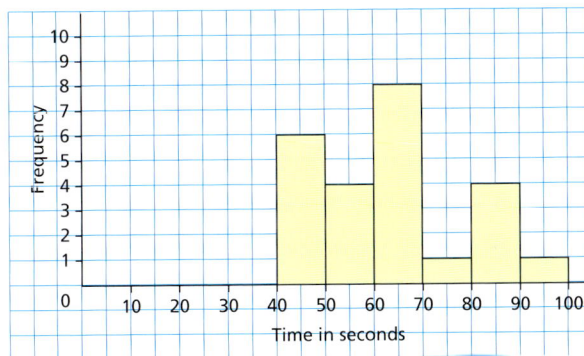

a) Without doing any calculations, write down two comments about the data.

b) Describe how you think the data was collected and who was asked.

c) Say what you think the raw data could have looked like for each class.

d) One of Ms Linnecor's students starts to work out the mean, the median and the mode for her class. She's not sure whether this can actually be done. Try it and see what you think.

e) Which average (mean, median or mode) would you use to convince your teacher which class was best at estimating time?

f) What does the range tell you about how good the classes were at estimating time?

g) In reality TV shows like 'Big Brother' and 'I'm a Celebrity Get Me Out of Here', contestants are sometimes set a task to estimate a length of time. Usually the time frame is much longer, say 4 hours. Sketch a bar chart to show what the results might be for a group of 15 contestants asked to estimate 4 hours.

Hypothesis: Children watch far too much TV

11 80 children and 100 adults on their way into the cinema were asked to say how many hours of TV they had watched in the last 24 hours. The tables below show the results of this survey:

Adults (over 18)	
Hours of TV watched (t)	Frequency
$0 \leq t < 1$	31
$1 \leq t < 2$	23
$2 \leq t < 3$	17
$3 \leq t < 4$	15
$4 \leq t < 6$	9
$6 \leq t < 8$	4
$8 \leq t < 24$	1

Children (under 18)	
Hours of TV watched (t)	Frequency
$0 \leq t < 1$	14
$1 \leq t < 2$	20
$2 \leq t < 3$	22
$3 \leq t < 4$	16
$4 \leq t < 6$	3
$6 \leq t < 8$	4
$8 \leq t < 24$	1

a) Imagine that you were the person collecting the data. Draw what you think your data collecting sheet may have looked like.

b) Suggest some reasons why you think the data is presented grouped together.

c) Find estimates for the mean, the median, the range and the modal class. Use these and your own experiences to write a paragraph commenting on the amount of television watched by children compared with adults.

d) Abi says: 'You can't compare this data because fewer children were asked than adults.' Does it matter that the person collecting the data asked fewer children than adults?

Now answer the questions in Workbook exercise 4.4 on pages 50–51 of your workbook.

Summary

This chapter has been about looking at data and how it is presented, then making calculations and finally drawing conclusions from the data.

For example, in a survey to find out how many matches were in a box, the matches in 20 boxes were counted. The results were:

38, 41, 40, 40, 41, 43, 39, 42, 40, 39, 44, 43, 41, 38, 39, 44, 45, 37, 44, 41

When the data is presented in this way, we usually say it is **raw data**.

To calculate the mean, we would find the total number of matches and share them out equally between all 20 boxes. So: 819/20 = 40.95

To find the median, we would firstly order the numbers and then find the middle value. In this case, because there are 20 numbers, we look at the 10th and 11th values, both of which are 41, so the median is 41.

Often, instead of presenting the data as raw data, we present it in a **frequency table**:

Number of matches	Number of boxes
37	1
38	2
39	3
40	3
41	4
42	1
43	2
44	3
45	1

We now have to be more careful when finding the mean, and it usually helps to imagine the data before it was put into a table. So here it would be:

37, 38, 38, 39, 39, 39, 40, 40, 40, 41, 41, 41, 41, 42, 43, 43, 44, 44, 44, 45

We can then find the mean and median in the same way.

Sometimes, particularly if there is a lot of data, a **grouped frequency table** will be used. Although we probably wouldn't use one for the data here, if we did it would look like:

Number of matches	Number of boxes
37–39	6
40–42	8
43–45	6

If we didn't know what the raw data looked like, all we could do now is estimate the mean. We would imagine the first six boxes as having 38 matches each, the next eight as having 41 each, and the last six as having 44 each.

This would give a total of 820 to share between the 20 boxes, so a mean of exactly 41.

Is it fair?

1 In PSHE a Year 11 class were discussing the death penalty for people convicted of murder. Some of the class were in favour of it and others were against it. They decided to ask other students in their school.

Some of the class asked the question like this:

> **Question A**
>
> The Bible says: 'An eye for an eye, a tooth for a tooth'.
>
> *Do you think that someone who murders another person should lose their own life?*

   a) What would your answer to this question be?

   b) What percentage of people do you think would say 'Yes' to this question?

Other students in the class asked the question this way:

> **Question B**
>
> The Bible teaches us the importance of forgiveness.
>
> *Do you think anyone has the right to take the life of another human being, whatever they have done?*

   c) What would your answer to this question be?

   d) What percentage of people do you think would say 'Yes' to this question?

e) The results of the survey were as follows:

	Yes	No
Question A	76%	24%
Question B	31%	69%

What do these results tell you about the students' opinions about the death penalty?

f) Rewrite the question so it is fair.

> If people's opinions are needed,
> it is important that the questions
> asked are fair.
> If a question favours a certain
> answer it is said to be **biased**.

Student's Book exercise 5.1

All of the following questions are biased. For each question, say why it is biased and write an unbiased version.

1 Don't you agree that football is the best sport?

2 There are many people that enjoy playing computer games. Are you one of them?

3 You don't like Olly Murs, do you?

4 Do you want to have more choice in the canteen rather than the usual menu?

5 I like shopping, don't you?

Are you old enough?

2 During the next PSHE lesson the students were discussing laws on the ages when young people are allowed to buy alcohol, buy cigarettes, vote in elections and leave school. They decided to ask as many students in the school as they could before the next lesson. They also wanted to know some background information on the students.

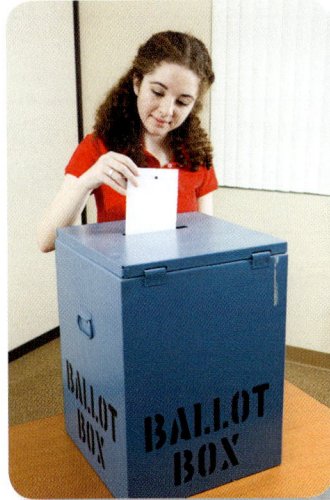

These are the questions that they asked:

A) How old are you?

B) What is your gender?

C) Do you smoke?

D) Do you drink alcohol?

E) At what age do you think you should be allowed to drink alcohol?

F) At what age do you think you should be allowed to smoke?

G) At what age do you think you should be allowed to leave school?

H) At what age do you think you should be allowed to vote in an election?

a) Think about how you would answer these questions. Can you think of any problems that there might be when answering them?

b) Which of the questions are finding out 'background' information?

c) Why do you think it might be important to have background information?

3 Here are some of the answers to the questionnaire:

A) How old are you?

> 12¾ 13 14 12 11½ 12 18 17 16 17 15 16 18 17 12½ 15 14 14 12
> 13¾ 13 13½ 15 14 14 16 16 11 15

B) What is your gender?

> F M F F M M F F F F M M M F M M M F F F F M F F M M F M F

C) Do you smoke?

> Y Occasionally N N Y N N Occasionally N N N N Y Y Sometimes
> N Socially N Occasionally N N Occasionally Y N N N Sometimes
> N Socially

D) Do you drink alcohol?

> N N Y Y Occasionally N N Y Y N N Occasionally Y Y Occasionally N
> Y Occasionally Y N N Y Sometimes N Sometimes N N Y N N

E) At what age do you think you should be allowed to drink alcohol?

> 16 16 18 21 20 15 Never 18 15 18 21 20 15 14 12 18 17 18 18 19 18
> 16 16 14 18 18 21 Never 16

F) At what age do you think you should be allowed to smoke?

> 18 16 Never 14 18 18 21 20 Never 18 18 15 14 14 18 Never 16 18
> 21 25 Never 14 12 Never 17 18 16 16 14

G) At what age do you think you should be allowed to leave school?

> 16 18 18 16 15 14 17 12 16 12 17 18 18 16 16 16 14 16 16 16 18 18
> 16 14 18 16 16 18 16

H) At what age do you think you should be allowed to vote in an election?

> 14 16 16 16 16 16 18 18 14 15 16 16 16 18 18 18 21 20 16 20 16 21
> 18 16 16 14 16 14 16

a) Information or data that is collected in person (like in this question) is called **primary data**. Why do you think it is called primary data?

b) Another type of data is called **secondary data**. What do you think that might be?

4 Charlotte thinks Question A ('How old are you?') is a good question because you find out the exact age of all the people completing the questionnaire.

Rachel thinks it would be easier to analyse if 'How old are you?' was followed by tick boxes, for example:

$11 \leq$ age < 14 ☐

$14 \leq$ age < 16 ☐

$16 \leq$ age < 18 ☐

a) Write down an advantage of using tick boxes after questions.

b) If you were 14 years old, which box would you tick?

c) If you were 13¾ years old, which box would you tick?

d) What would be the advantage of using tick boxes for Question C, 'Do you smoke?'

5 Rachel decides to have five tick boxes for the question 'Do you smoke?' Here are the first two options:

Never ☐

$1 \leq$ cigarettes per week < 21 ☐

a) Write down what you think the other three tick box options could be.

b) Write down five tick box options for Question D, 'Do you drink alcohol?'

c) Do you think 'Do you drink alcohol?' is a good question? What does the question *not* allow you to find out?

> **Types of data**
> There can be different types of information:
> **Qualitative** data is non-numerical data, e.g. your gender.
> **Discrete** data is countable data, e.g. the number of cigarettes someone smokes.
> **Continuous** data is data that you measure, e.g. your age or how tall you are.

Turn to page 52 of your workbook and complete the table in Workbook exercise 5.1.

X-Factor

6 At Kingswood High School the students were X-Factor mad. At the start of November 2011, a Year 11 class did a survey to find out who they thought would win and who they thought would be next to be eliminated. They asked their friends within the school. These are the top five results:

Act	% of students who thought they would win
Little Mix	24%
The Risk	23%
Misha B	21%
Janet Davlin	15%
Craig Colton	10%

Act	% of students who thought they would be eliminated
Johnny Robinson	41%
Kitty Brucknell	26%
Frankie Cocozza	14%
Janet Davlin	6%
Misha B	6%

On Sunday 6 November 2011, the two acts that had the lowest number of votes were eliminated. They were Johnny Robinson (a thin middle-aged man) and The Risk (five good-looking men, aged about 20).

Try to explain why The Risk got the lowest number of votes from viewers but were second top in the students' vote. Why did the two votes not give the same results? Discuss your ideas with a partner.

7 It was revealed in a national newspaper that the people who vote in the X-Factor are:
- 25% girls aged 7–14
- 25% women aged 35–50
- 25% people aged 51–65
- 25% others

a) What do you think 'others' means?

b) Explain in detail how the Year 11 students could get a better idea of who will be voted off next. Who exactly should they ask?

Summary

In this chapter you have been introduced to a number of key ideas.

Bias in questions
We have seen how questions can be biased. For example: 'Maths is easily your favourite subject, isn't it?' is not a fair question as it encourages you to agree.

Response boxes
These make the question easier to answer and easier to analyse. For example:

What is your favourite subject?

Maths	☐	PE	☐
English	☐	RE	☐
Science	☐	Other	☐

Primary data
Primary data is data you collect yourself.

Secondary data
Secondary data is obtained from published sources (e.g. the internet). It is data that already exists so it is second-hand.

Types of data

There can be different types of information:
- **Qualitative** data is non-numerical data, e.g. your favourite subject.
- **Discrete** data is countable data, e.g. number of maths lessons per week.
- **Continuous** data is data that you measure, e.g. how long you spend on your maths homework.

Bias in who is asked
To get a proper idea of what people think you must be careful to ask a full range of people. For example, if you first asked the top maths set and then the bottom maths set what their favourite subject is, you may get different answers.